GETTING EVERYTHING YOU WANT

YOUR GUIDE TO WEALTH, SUCCESS, RELATIONSHIPS, HAPPINESS & LOVE

By Mary Lou Morris

P.O. Box 888
Libby, MT 59923
email: onestepclosermt@juno.com

Cover Photo by Mary Lou Morris

Published by RUSA, Inc.
Redmond, Oregon

ISBN 1-888368-05-5

DEDICATION

To my husband, Curt, whom the angels
sent to be my guardian on earth, and who
has always supported me even when
he did not understand me.

To my dogs, both past and present,
Billee, Jessie, Molly, and Libby,
who lovingly taught me about unconditional
love and what it means to live exquisitely
in the present.

All of you have filled my heart and soul.
I am eternally grateful and love you deeply.

How can I try to explain, cause when I do
he turns away again.
It's always been the same, same old story.
From the moment I could talk, I was ordered to listen,
Now there's a way and I know that I have to go.
Away, I know, I have to go...
If they were right I'd agree,
but it's them they know, not me
Now there's a way, and I know that I have to go away,
I know I have to go.

Cat Stevens

TABLE OF CONTENTS

INTRODUCTION

"When I find myself in times of trouble, Mother Mary comes to me, whispering words of wisdom. Let It Be...
And in my hour of darkness there is still a light that shines on me...There will be an answer. Let It Be..."

John Lennon & Paul McCartney

If you have picked up this book to read, then you are among those of us who are searching for answers or solutions. One of us who somehow has been led to a place where we want alternatives to what the masses are experiencing. One who wants to feel we have some control over what direction our lives are going. One who feels there are answers other than what we were perhaps brought up to believe. Or perhaps you have already found your way and just want to read another book on the subject. I have found that as I re-read a book or a new book on the same subject, that as time passes and I reach higher levels of consciousness, I see things from a different perspective, catch things I missed before, and enhance what I already know. Whatever brought you here, welcome!

I have been aware of my journey to my Self for sometime now, but as I look back on my life I realize that it started long before I was aware of it. Sometimes I feel like a novice at this and then I remember back a few years, sometimes not even that far, like maybe only last year, and I see how much I have grown and how much better my life flows. And I expect that next year, and the next, I will feel the same. I have evolved tremendously from where I was as part of the mass mind of wrong thinking. I have found that my journey to spirit is not a destination, but a journey of discoveries and growth. It is an ever-expanding evolution and rediscovery of who I really am and where I came from, what I am here for, and where I will end up: a story with a vague outline and no set text. Living within a set text will strangle the very life out of you. So don't try to write the whole book of how your life will be. Write one page at a time. Perhaps even just one sentence at a time. Leave yourself open for the unexpected. That is where the adventure of life comes from.

Perhaps our journey can be viewed as a trip. We have many destinations on our trip. There will be places we want to stop and sightsee. When I first became aware of my spiritual growth I thought, "This is great. I'll read these books and listen to these tapes, learn all this stuff and then I'll be all knowing and have all these wondrous things happen. My life will be easy and I'll be rich." Well, though it is all true, none of it is untrue, what I have found is that I have stops along the way and some sightseeing to do. It's all part of the journey, part of our growth.

Getting fulfillment and affluence into our life is not going out and doing a few things here and there and then "poof" it's all there. It is a journey we take along with all its detours. We can call them lessons. Where you are in your evolution and how much effort you put into it will determine your path. If you are looking for enlightenment, if you want to call it that, or seeking more in your life, you have to go out there and get it. It's not going to come to you, slap you upside the head and say, "Here I am. Let's make your life wonderful." You need to make your own commitment and then follow through.

We are programmed in our upbringing to 'fit in'. If you find yourself not fitting in, it's okay. There's no need to struggle. Just accept that what everyone else is doing is not your cup of tea and go about your own life. Those of like minds will be drawn to you and you will establish a new community of friends. These people will lift you up and encourage you, rather than put you down and tell you you're nuts. It is best to maintain a certain level of secrecy when on your spiritual quest in order to protect the power you are connecting to. Friends of like mind and beliefs will assist you along your journey. I am talking about those outside this circle. Anyone or anything that pushes negative energy at you can steal your power, can make you doubt yourself. I am not saying to avoid those who do not follow your path. I am saying it is best not to share what you are doing with them. Until you are a master of your own world, their negative views and comments will rob you of your self-confidence. Also, be aware that your own boastful attitude, which comes from ego, will only hurt you. Become humble in your newfound strength and insights.

It is not my intention to put down any other belief systems because I believe that what is being offered here can work with many of them. In fact, it is a part of some of them, only some have been lost, misinterpreted, misunderstood or simply overlooked for a while. If I may paraphrase a little from the Bible: *All things whatsoever you pray for and ask for, if you believe you shall receive them, you will receive them* and Jesus said of his work, *this you shall do and even more.* This ideal life we are searching for has been called *The Promised Land, The Fifth World Of Peace, Nirvana,* the *New Dream*, the *Infinite Self, Heaven,* and by many other names. We can call it what we like, the feeling and wisdom we are seeking is the same.

In this book I intend to show you why and how you got to where you are now. This is not to presume you are in a bad place. Hopefully, many of you are in a good place and just want to be even better. I want to share with you what I have learned from my teachers, my experiences, and my connection with spirit. It is my desire to touch each of you in the way that you need at this time to move forward in your life and to 'experience your best'.

There's an expression that states: *Teachers cannot teach us. They can only remind us of what we already know.*

CHAPTER ONE

Happiness Cannot Wait

There are many pieces and parts to the process of spiritual evolution. We all go about it from different places and directions. What I have learned is that nothing else really works like it could unless we 'get happy'. For all of you fun loving guys and gals, that doesn't mean external or artificial stimulation – those are pleasure and we'll talk about that later. I'm talking about the kind of happiness that comes from inside you. The kind of happiness that comes from love, appreciation of our world, and connection to spirit.

We need to take the time *each* day to honor ourselves. Just a little time if that's all you can spare. If some days all you have is a few minutes, that's fine. But spending at least 20 minutes gives you the opportunity to reach the desired state of relaxation and allow for your connection to spirit. Go to a place where you can be alone to experience silence and just *being*. I call this meditation, but if that's not your thing, just put on some beautiful music, close your eyes and quiet the mind. You can call it whatever you like. Every so often you might try a nice warm bath as part of this experience, or sitting in a hot tub under the stars. Turning off the chatter in the head is no easy task, so don't get discouraged if at first this is a struggle. There is a part of you that will chirp in with things like "Don't forget the toilet paper next time you go shopping!" or "Did I remember to pay the insurance?" Just keep coming back to the quiet each time you catch your mind jabbering on. You can answer with something like "Thank you so much. Now go away and leave me alone till I ask for you." Even after you have been at this for a long time there are times when the mind wants to have its say. Don't worry. It's normal. It's ego trying to be in control. But be assured that until you are willing to take this time and make a commitment to yourself that this is one of the most important aspects of your day; even if you are enthusiastic now, it will not last. The only way to connect to your inner Self, Higher Self, spirit, God-Self, whatever you have named the *real* you, is through silence, the quieting of the mind, the chatter.

Let's talk about ego for a minute. By my definition ego is

that part of you that is 'the programming' from your upbringing. It is that voice in your head that never shuts up. It is that part of you that runs your life according to what you have been taught your life ought to be by those around you. It is that part of you that is always telling you what to think, how to react, what's right and what's wrong. It's been a part of you from day one. It is not about to let you go messing with things without a struggle. It likes things the way they are. It feels safe when it is in control. It thrives on control and fear. These are the only things it knows. It has been programmed to operate in this fashion. It will interrupt you any time it feels the old ways, the safe ways, are being threatened. It will disguise itself to have you think it is spirit. It is very clever. Learning to distinguish the two can be a challenge in itself. The best way to tell who you are listening to is to focus on the heart area and sense the feeling there. If it feels loving, gentle, without pressure, then it is probably spirit. Time and experience will assist you. Even if we learn new teachings that we know in our hearts are more likely to bring happiness and fulfillment in our lives, our ego is going to fight to preserve what it already knows and is comfortable with. To heck if those new teachings are good for us or not. It is going to try every trick it can to get you to stay in your comfort zone. You have to really want to have your personal power restored in order for it to happen.

So most of us, being raised with beliefs we find to be contrary to what we are now discovering to be the truths about ourselves, are in the process of undoing this programming. Our journey through this lifetime is to transcend those old beliefs and come to live in the truth – we are all spiritual beings that are here to have human experiences, not humans who have occasional spiritual experiences. We are a part of all-that-is, a part of the energy that flows through everything, a part of what I am going to call *God.* Different religions and belief systems around the world call it by different names, but it's all the same energy force. We are a part of it. We cannot be separated from it – which is what many, most, of us have been taught. It is this separation that causes us to feel lack in our lives – whether is be lack of money, achievement, knowledge, relationships, or fulfillment of any kind. This is where our ability to feel happy runs into a roadblock. What we fail to see is that everything is here for us. It is *already* here. What we are doing is going through the process of rediscovering this. We are searching for ways to align our energy with our desires. That is how creation works. Each of us has a different route to take and each route will take a different amount of time. So never, *never,* compare your journey with anyone else's. We all go along our own route to regain our true heritage and know our own truth. But then it's not enough just to know our truth, we have to live it. That's the hard part, because we have been conditioned for so long in the old ways.

From the day we are born into this life, we are exposed to other peoples' visions of how things are and should be. All of our choices are made for us. We go along because we are innocent and are so dependant on the adults. As we grow up we may disagree with some of the things we are being taught and we may rebel and say, "no", but for most of us we are still young and innocent enough that their visions of how things are become *our* visions. Without even knowing it, we are handed a life that we haven't even had a choice in. It is a life based on fear and giving up our control to others. That's not to say we should blame our parents or teachers or friends or church. They are all just doing what they have been 'programmed' to do. They don't mean any harm. In fact, they think they're doing the right thing. But these are *their* visions, not ours. And for the most part, their beliefs are based on lies. Lies set up to take control of our free-thinking minds.

All of this started long before our lifetimes. It started long, long ago. Priests attacked independent thinking and the oneness of man to God, believing that this type of consciousness undermined their authority and power. And so began the dogma of directing individuals to look outside of themselves for their salvation. In around 180 A.D. the Bishop of Lyons set forth his "Five Books Against Heresies" choosing only what supported his demands. Many others throughout history edited and interpreted ancient writings to suit their purposes of control. Many sacred texts had to be kept secret for centuries in order to preserve them. Around 400 this planet entered into a thousand year period known as the "Dark Ages" where very few advances were made in human evolution due to the restrictions placed on individual thinking and beliefs. The church leaders controlled spiritual enlightenment. Which meant there was none. When the church wasn't in control, government was. It wasn't until around the 1500's that the lost teachings began to resurface on any significant scale. We are still trying to re-establish our *true selves* today.

You put all these visions together, past and present, and you get what I call the *world vision.* Who says we have to agree? Are you satisfied with the way our world is today? The way to change it is one person at a time. That is what we are here for. But the ego is going to fight for the world vision, so be prepared and be patient. The more we are able to connect with spirit, the more control our true Self will have. This will allow more love in our lives – love that comes from the inside and love we are willing to receive from our world. And love is happiness.

Whether it comes from India, the East, the early tribes of the Americas, "ancient" or "modern", teachings from all over the world come from the same truth. They teach about claiming our divinity and finding the god, or power within. They teach about having our hearts open and becoming wise. We are alive because we are a part of God. We are a part of everything there is. God runs through everything. We are all connected to each other and everything else. It is the spirit, the power, that part of God that makes us alive.

If we are truly a part of God, why don't we know it? We don't know it because we have been programmed not to know. We have been taught over the centuries that this power is outside of ourselves, that we must look somewhere else other than ourselves. Our awareness of the force within has been taken away in order to control us, limit us, and keep us in fear in order to keep this control over us. But we are truly powerful. We are what we believe. We were taught from the day we were born. We were put into a box and told who we are and because we were innocent and believed it, that is what we became.

If we were able to become what we thought we were, then we are able to become what we *really* are, once we know it and understand it. This reminds me of a Disney movie I saw recently, "The Other Me". A boy accidentally clones himself and in order to skip school sends his clone in his place. It turns out this clone can do almost anything, gets great grades and becomes very popular at school, whereas the real boy is shy and reserved and his grades are marginal. The same genes, the same person only the new boy had not had any "head trips" laid on him, no programming and was completely uninhibited to seek out his own potential, which he found to be limitless. It was a great show! I loved it.

Now it is our time, because we are no longer innocent and can think on our own, to step away and take a look for ourselves...to see we are limitless...to realize our own power. It's there. It always has been. In touching spirit this way, by re-connecting with our God-Self, we regain our happiness.

Another way to connect with spirit is to spend time in nature. To observe what a miracle Mother Earth is. The varying landscapes, the ever-changing skies, and the beauty of the rain and snow take my breath away. Being in nature puts us in touch with that part of us that is also a part of all creation and we begin to see the perfection in all of it. This communion with who we really are brings love into our very being. We need to take time whenever possible to make this connection with nature. If you are city-bound, then go to a park on a regular basis to just sit and be still. Also schedule regular trips out into the countryside. You will not regret a single trip. Nature is an essential part of what we are. Take the time to look outside everyday. Catch a glimpse of what is being presented to you. In fact, take a look as many times as you like!!

We will find through these practices, which will become our new habits, that there is more happiness in every aspect of our lives. When we are happy everything else flows smoother and things are easier to accomplish. We will also have more control over our reactions to the world outside of us. We will get into how we become a master at this later. For now it is enough to know that we need not be a bundle of programmed responses. That is a part of our old programming. We are building new programs. Our new program allows us to be compassionate and yet not be attached to that which is not a part of our being. We need not let old emotional wounds affect us today. We can heal those wounds and see a new vision for our world. With this healing comes the ability to observe what used to upset us from a new prospective and therefore be able to respond in a way that doesn't add stress to our lives. So even though the world around us doesn't seem to change much, our place in it and our actions in it do. Even though things will still come along that are distressing, we will be better able to handle them. Our world need not be an emotional roller coaster. We can remain in our new world vision while the rest of the world is still in the old world vision. We can find more happiness in each moment.

We have come into human form for spirit to experience *humanness* – emotions, the senses, lineal time. Though spirit is here to experience all of this, spirit has also come here to bring some *heaven to earth.* So that as humans we can experience the graces of heaven, or whatever you would like to call it. We mustn't beat ourselves up in our striving to be more spiritual when we go through the human emotions and what it is to be human. Part of the reason spirit is here is to experience all that stuff. And then part of the reason is also to allow us, as the physical part of our being, to bring divinity into our physical experience. And that is what we are all looking for. Call it what ever you want. We want to experience peace and love –both giving and receiving. We want to experience flow, abundance, to have a desire and have it show up for us.

So many of us live our lives under the thought pattern of, "When I accomplish this, then I can have that" or "When this happens then I'll be happy" or "When I have x amount of dollars I will relax and enjoy my life." It's always when I accomplish such and such then I can have what I really want. You'll wait a whole lifetime and never achieve fulfillment coming at it from that direction. We must come from "I am going to take time each day to find fulfillment in my life where I am right now". No matter where you are in your life there is beauty and love all around you if you know how and where to find it. There is happiness in the smallest of things. We are going expand on this, so read on.

CHAPTER TWO

Allowing Ourselves To Receive

In order to receive the abundance and all the good things in life we are wanting, we must first allow this to happen. How do we do this? First, as discussed in the previous chapter we have to find happiness in where we are now, while still intending for our desires to materialize for us. I hesitate to state, 'second', because what we are going to discuss now is actually essential to our happiness. But as you continue to read this book you will find that though I have tried to put an order to some of this information, a lot of it overlaps and sort of winds back and forth through each other. So hang in there with me and we will have a clear path by the end.

Where were we going with this? Oh yeah! Love. You cannot truly love others until you are able to love yourself. Now your ego may be telling you, "Hey! I'm great. How can you even consider that I don't love myself?" But as I explained about the ego, it will tell you anything to remain in control. Then there will be other egos out there saying, "Of course I don't love myself. Look at what a schmuck I am!" It is still your ego running your program. So how do we go about loving ourselves, *really*, loving ourselves?

First of all you must accept yourself as the divine being that you are, and as the human being that you are. You are a part of God and if you love God, which is all of life and everything that we perceive, then allow yourself to love yourself as well. As divine beings we are love. All we need do is to allow the expression of our true Self. In order to do this we must heal the wounds from our up bringing. Focusing on yourself is not selfish. It is self-love. It is selfish only when there is *no* self-love and your focus on yourself is to protect yourself from others. If you love yourself, you will not need protection.

If you lack confidence and self-esteem, just accept that as part of you now, but then move beyond it. If you try to fight it, you put energy into it. Ignore any traits you find limiting. What you put your attention on expands and what you ignore withers and is soon gone. So ignore what you don't want and concentrate on what you do. Another emotion that holds us back is guilt. It is used by others and your ego to control you. That's all it is – a way to control. It is based on rules others made with control specifically in mind. It is up to you to decide the rules for your own life. When you are with spirit those rules will always be liberating and never impose pain.

Now let's work on forgiveness. Anything that you have experienced that you are beating yourself up about is in the past. It cannot be changed. It was a part of your journey. Part of the lessons you are here to learn. What you can do is learn the lesson that it provided you and move onto a new level of experience. A quick note here: if you do not learn your lesson the first time, the lesson will keep showing up in your life in one form or another until you do. So pay attention in your life! Take stock of the things that seem to keep re-occurring and find the message, the reason, and the solution. This is the way you can move on.

Make a list of those whom you wish to forgive and whom you wish forgiveness from. Go into your silence, or prayers, and allow spirit to express its love for you. Then while in silence, reach out to those who may be a part of it and forgive them and allow their spirit to forgive you. Send your love to that person or situation and know forgiveness is there. Then forgive yourself. Actually, spirit to spirit, the forgiveness happened at the moment of the event, but this is a way for you to formalize it in your mind. Know that forgiveness has taken place. Now if you want to and it would make it more effective for you, you can actually contact those people whom you wish forgiveness from, and simply ask them to forgive you. Be forewarned though, that even though you may be open to making things right, to this type of cleansing, they may not and it can open up wounds full of infected emotions. So unless you are fully prepared for the consequences, perhaps this is not the path to choose. If you are, good for you! In any event, when it comes right down to it, you have nothing to forgive yourself for. But it makes us feel better if we do. And it is a way for us to allow ourselves self-love. This is where your healing is going to come from. Someone can forgive you to your face, but unless you also forgive yourself, it's still going to haunt you. Another very important point to make here is that you cannot truly forgive others until you can forgive yourself, just as you cannot truly love others until you love yourself.

Before we move on I would like to say that this process of going within works for any problem or situation you may face. You do not have to confront things head on. Go within and visualize a peaceful solution, send love to that person or situation, know it is done. Then just wait and go about your business. The more you do this and see the results you can get, the more confident you will become of your own personal power. Whatever your hang-up, the solution is internal and the healing is internal. It does no good to look outside of yourself.

This leads us into judgment. Something we do all the time without even thinking about it, an essential part of our programming. Constantly in our minds we are categorizing sounds, our surrounding, others and ourselves. God is not that great being that sits up in his kingdom and watches over us, passing judgment as to whether what we do is good or bad, right or wrong. God has no judgment, no emotion. God is a pervasive spirit, an omniscient energy that runs through all things and is made up of complete and unconditional love. There is no judgment. And yet we somehow have decided that we must judge everything. Everything is compared, graded, and put into neat little categories. We don't even need all the facts, to know those involved, or have the necessary knowledge to make these judgments. Others taught us what and how things should be. If it does not meet our 'approval' it is bad and if it does then it's good. We even accept our judgments second hand from others through gossip and the news.

Most of us were raised on the basis of fear and self-rejection if we do not behave in a certain manner. We are compared to that which would be *perfect*. So we end up trying to find that "perfectness" in ourselves, others, and everything else. What we fail to realize is that everything is already perfect in the moment. Our image of what is perfect is based on misconceptions and misunderstanding. What we have been taught is perfect does not exist. God doesn't put us here and then allow for some good and some bad. We come here into this human form with all the essential knowledge and tools. It is up to us whether we find our Selves and how we use our time here.

The act of judging takes an enormous amount of our energy. Just think about how busy our minds are all the time constantly chattering on and on about this and that: worrying about things that have already happened, things that might happen, and classifying everything. If we can learn to catch ourselves each time we start to judge, we can start to use that energy to bring more of what we want into our lives- abundance, love and peace. This is essential. Make a commitment right here and now and every morning and each time you catch yourself, that "from now on I will not judge."

If we love ourselves, forgive ourselves, and stop judging ourselves, then from that point we can work on not judging what is going on around us. When you judge and reject others, know you are also rejecting yourself, for we are all part of the same. When you judge and reject that which is outside of you, you also reject yourself. When you reject yourself, you reject the spirit within.

Now let us discuss responsibility. We are only responsible for our half of all our relationships. I know many of us would love to control it all, but if you haven't figured out yet that you cannot, then *figure it out now!!* Stop beating your head against the wall. It hurts! And not just yourself. Do your best in all situations with the knowledge that you have to draw from, and with the love you have inside. That's all there is. Just do your very best and if by chance you screw it up, forgive yourself, learn from it, do better in the future, but move on. You are half of the equation in all relationships whether it is with other humans, animals, or the environment. You only need to take care of your half of it. Fill it with love, respect and gentleness. If we were all just responsible for ourselves: being happy, full of love, taking care of our little space on the planet, and keeping our noses out of where they do not belong. If we would use all the energy we waste judging and trying to control what we cannot, can you even imagine what our world might be like? With each of us doing so, what our planet could be like?

Before you can live a life of true happiness and abundance

you have to heal the emotional wounds that you have gathered during your lifetime. This can be accomplished by working on forgiveness, judgment and self-love. You can be receiving all the love in the world from the outside and you will still not be happy or fulfilled. The love needs to come from the inside. Until you are full of love inside and you love from the inside out, you will always be crippled. When you love yourself first, all the rest comes naturally. If you are full of love, loving life and loving everything around you, everything else will just fall into place. Then there is no way you will fail, no way you will not be happy and no way you will not experience the power that is your birthright. It is this power we use to manifest abundance into our lives. It is love, including forgiveness and gratitude, which opens us to this flow, this power. It is knowing we deserve it. It is my intention to assist you in retrieving your personal power so let's move on.

CHAPTER THREE

Your Words Form Your World

Most of us don't like the idea that what we are living is of our own creation. Ego would much rather blame someone or something else when things are not to our liking and take all the credit when they are. I cannot begin to count the number of times I have heard something along the lines, "This is reality! We don't make this world, we just live in it. This is just the way things are!" Though it is true that we are stuck living here on this planet and we cannot control most of what is going on out there, it is not true that we are *stuck* with the way things are in our lives. Before we go any further you better just get used to it! *You did* create whatever your circumstances are. I know it may be very difficult for some of you to go along with that. But for those of you whose ego just wants to buck you some on this, stay with us here and by the end of this book you will be much more open.

So how does this all happen? How does creation work? It is all energy seeking to be manifest from unmanifest. There are books that go into this quite thoroughly and explain it from spiritual points of view and scientific points of view and the basics are the same. So we agree on this point: all of creation is made up of energy and information. I will go into this a bit more later on. Right now I want to talk about how our words create our experiences.

Have you heard the expression, "You are what you eat?" Well, you are also what you think about. Take notice of the people around you. Those who are negative, complain a lot, and seem to always have a *bee in their bonnet,* experience one misfortune after another. Those who are upbeat, generous with their time and themselves, and keep a positive attitude experience more good fortune in their lives. Now there is probably someone reading this and thinking, "Well, I know so and so and they were really upbeat and they just died of cancer." Don't presume to know what that person really thought about everyday or what their purpose here was. Don't confuse that with what I'm trying get across. What we think and believe is what comes to us. All of creation is vibration. Like attracts like. So if you don't want poop in your life, get your mind out of the toilet. What you think about is what you get in some form or another.

It all starts with your word. Thoughts, your internal dialog, are made up of words, so let's concentrate on the importance of the word. Think about how powerful words are. Words in the form of a compliment can lift you up and words in the form of an insult or attack can break your heart. Words were used to program you as you grew up. They are used to instill compliance. They are thrown around without regard. Words are our power. We can use them to raise our world to a higher level or to tear it down. Unfortunately they are used for the latter more often. We can start to change this by starting with ourselves. We can make a commitment that from now on we are going to be aware of our words and choose them carefully. We are going to start paying attention to our internal dialog and editing negative words by changing them every time we catch ourselves using our words in a negative manner. We are also going to start thinking before we speak so we will be sure what comes out of our mouths is kind and thoughtful. So many times our responses come out of habit and conditioning. We have buttons that can be pushed! We don't even think about what we say. We just open our mouths and out pours all this garbage. Half the time we don't even mean what comes out. The other half we have to work on because we should only say that which comes from our hearts, not our egos. As we evolve and regain our lost knowledge, we find our hearts and the use of our word to hurt others is not a part of who we are. So we will continue to make this a conscious part of every moment until we have broken our old habit of thoughtless talk and have our new habit of being honorable with our word. As we police our thoughts, we will find it easier to police our spoken word as well.

Our spoken word. What do we use it for? To communicate. But have you stopped to notice that over 90% of our spoken words are about nonsense! Most of what we talk about has nothing to do with ourselves and most of it is none of our business in the first place. My parents used to always say, "If you don't have something nice to say, then say nothing at all." (I wish they had remembered that when they were bawling me out about something I had done to displease them! (Just joking Mom and Dad. I love you!) I would like to expound on that with, "If you aren't asked, don't say anything, and if you are asked and it has nothing to do with you personally, don't say anything, and even if it does have something to do with you only answer if it can in some way help them out." And even then don't presume to tell people what to do, just head them off in the right direction to find their own answers.

We do ourselves and others a great disservice when we make idle conversation about others or spread rumors. It is not honoring our word to speak unkindly, to judge, or use our word in anyway to get back at someone. It doesn't matter who or what they have done. It is not our place or our business to engage in such conversation. It places negative energy around our own spirit and everything around us. We use our word to create negativity when it is our goal to live peacefully and gracefully. How can you expect to attract abundance into your life (which is positive energy) if you surround yourself with such negativity? You must be willing to make a commitment to be honorable with your word if you intend to find success, abundance and all the good things in life flowing to you.

By placing honor on our word we find a lot of the strife and stress in our lives melts away. We have fewer confrontations, people react to us differently and our world starts to be more harmonious and to have a natural flow to it. Because we are conscious of our thoughts we can now spend more of our time thinking about what we want, more time appreciating things around us, and indeed, appreciating ourselves, and less time letting the mind go on and one with it's endless chatter, most of which is negative, judgmental, and centers on worrying about what we *do not* want to happen. This brings us back to creating through our thoughts (which is what we do) thus we create a better world for ourselves because our thoughts and words are from our hearts.

To summarize it all again, and we cannot go over this too much because in my opinion this is such a huge part of what we create for ourselves: We do create our world through our beliefs, which come from our up bringing and what we choose to pick up later on in life. Like what we are working on here – replacing those beliefs that do not serve our higher good and are basically based on lies with new beliefs based our own truth and our own power. Our beliefs run around in our minds in the form of words. This is our way of communicating with ourselves. The structure and content of these sentences playing in our head give off vibrations and these vibrations attract like vibrations. So we get what we think about. Let's make a note here also that the universe doesn't use complete sentences when receiving orders from us. It just picks up the key words and goes from there. So it does not recognize "no" or "don't". So to think, "I don't want lack in my life" is heard as "Lack in my life". Or to put it another way, when you think in this form you are thinking about lack. And Presto! You get lack. We must always think about what we *do* want and *not* think about what we do not want.

By not being conscious of our spoken word we put off negative energy or vibrations when we are not honorable with our words. In doing so we attract more negative energy and thus find ourselves in situations we would prefer not to be in. By making an effort to police our spoken word and our thoughts we bring them into our consciousness and just in doing so we begin to be in control of our own world. The more we do it, the better we become at it and then our old habits are broken and replaced with a new habit that brings harmony and flow into our lives. That is what spirit wants for us. All the good things in life.

CHAPTER FOUR

Acknowledging the Power Within

"It is not necessary for even one other person to understand the Laws of the Universe or the processes that we are offering here in order for you to have a wonderful, happy, productive Life Experience – for you are the attractor of your experience. Just you!" *-Abraham Hicks*

We are in the habit of looking outside of ourselves for our needs. It is natural. When we were children we were dependant on the outside world for our survival. Now we need to realize that not only is everything we need and want already here, but that we all have equal access to it and an equal right to it. The source of everything that shows up in our lives is within us. That energy that manifests the universe is also in each of us. We are a part of it all, a part of God. We have discussed creating our own world through our thoughts, our internal dialog. This is our way of communicating with the source of all-that-is. This source is a part of us. It is not outside ourselves. The more we discipline ourselves to honor who we are and change our negative habits, the more in touch with this power we become. It takes effort on our part to re-discover this part of our being. If you are not willing to generate energy on your own, of your own, then you might as well put this book down now. You have to at least be ready to explore the ideas (which you must be if you've gotten this far) and later on you will have to generate you own energy to connect to your source. This is done through the disciplines discussed in this book.

Hoping, believing isn't enough. You have to *know* your power. You have to experience it. It will be subtle, especially when you are first learning to recognize it. Pay attention for the slightest signs of it. It is there. It always has been. The more you acknowledge it, the stronger it will become. I need to interject a word of caution here. When I was first getting started I would get these "inspirations" and off I would go thinking spirit was leading me to greatness. Don't be fooled by the ego. Listen to your heart, not your head. Be smart. Don't beat yourself up about it when you end up with egg on your face. Just learn from it and move on. Your power is not about doing great, wondrous things, though some do. And that is wonderful. Your power is about you, whatever your purpose here is. It is about tapping into the source and having all that you want manifest into your experience. It is about acknowledging that you are more than this physical being.

This power within us lies there mostly dormant because we either don't realize we have it or don't know how to use it or both. Actually it is being used by us, but not to fulfill our dreams because we do not understand how it all works. So let's talk about our habits, patterns, and how this affects our ability to use this power to get what we truly want. We are all creatures of habit. We follow predictable patterns throughout most of our day. Much of what we do is done without much thought. And unfortunately, most of this is in complete conflict with our innermost desires. So why do we behave this way? Like I said, it is all just habit. We've already discussed some habits we need to change, but each of us has individual habits that are causing us distress in our lives. You must start to examine your own life, what works, what doesn't, what you like in it, what you do not and then work on changing things. We look to recognize patterns, to even realize them, and just in bringing them to our consciousness we are on our way to correcting those things that are not working in our lives. The more we are aware of our patterns or habits, the more we can catch ourselves repeating something we wish to change. Then we get to the point where we catch it just before we do it and replace whatever it is with what we feel is appropriate to our spiritual quest, and from there we develop our new habits.

From that point we are behaving in a manner that is supportive of our dreams. And this allows us to not only to conserve our energy for attracting our desires, but saves a lot of energy that was previously being wasted. This energy too can then be channeled into fulfilling our dreams and bringing more heaven to earth.

Habits that we have had for many years, perhaps a lifetime, are hard to break. Also, habits within a long-term relationship such as a spouse or your family are extremely difficult to deal with. Those buttons seem to be the most sensitive and easiest pushed, and to add to that, they are the hardest to ignore or get away from. It is not uncommon to find resistance from those close to you as you adopt new beliefs and want things to be different, unless you are blessed to have them along with you on your quest. Many times this is not the case and it can be very frustrating indeed. Just remember they are coming from their own fears and resistance to change. Try not to let them trigger your defenses. *It's hard! Believe me, I know.*

As you are establishing new points of view and where you will be coming from in this new experience, don't be hard on yourself when you find some habits difficult to overcome. Remember, part of the reason you are here is to learn the disciplines necessary for your evolution back to spirit. You are not expected to be perfect. The standards we use for perfection are set by our past conditioning. To God everything is already perfect. As humans we will experience times of disappointment with ourselves. I really want to make this point clear: *do not be disappointed* when you fall short of your goals or things don't turn out as great as you expected. Mark these things up as lessons and stepping-stones. We are here to experience it all and to evolve beyond it. With each stepping-stone you land on, another one will appear for you to move ahead on. As you proceed you experience less disappointment and in time you will no longer feel disappointment. It will no longer be a part of who you are. You will be an observer, detached and yet participating. You will trust that things are as they should be and good things are everywhere if you open your eyes. Also, be sure to acknowledge yourself, and give yourself an "atta boy!" when you do things right. It is up to you to take your blinders off and see your own Truth.

A lot of our behavior that uses up a great deal of our personal power stems from anger and /or fear. They are the same. We must come to the understanding that it is not what is happening, or what has been said, that causes us distress. It is *our reaction* to it. This, too, stems from our conditioning. Those people and things that push our buttons the most are our best teachers. They show us where our weaknesses still lie – what still needs our work. Your negative reactions arise from taking things personally. This is ego's reaction, not the reaction of your true Self. These reactions have been a part of us for so long. We learned them from our up bringing, from what we were taught and observed from others. We take everything so personally. As if we are so important that other people spend their time thinking about us. P-lease! Give me a break! Let's face it. In the world out there everyone is so caught up in their own lives, they don't give a tinker's damn about anyone else. What they say and do comes from their own fears and frustrations. You had nothing to do with it. They are only venting their own fears and anger. So what makes us think that what they are going through has anything to do with us? I'll tell you what. Ego, that's what; our own self-importance. We make the assumption that we know what their motivation is and blame it on ourselves. We actually believe we could be the cause of someone else's fears. And they actually believe we are in some cases. By the same token, don't go blaming anyone or something else for your fears and frustrations. Nor should you blame yourself. Just accept them. They are yours and yours alone and it is up to you to heal your own wounds and move on. Remember, we are only responsible for our half of every relationship or situation. These reactions are some of the habits we are changing. My advice is to avoid anger and negative emotions and those who display such traits. When caught in this situation, settle it quickly, let it go and get the hell out of there. As we continue to work on our half we will find ourselves in less such situations and our reactions will change also. When we come a place of self-love and inner peace and we understand why people behave as they do, we don't take such things to heart. There will no longer be so much distress and we will in turn be conserving our personal power. Instead of reacting, we learn to take appropriate action. Everyone wins when we can do this. Sure, things are going to happen, but we will not make it all our fault, all about our shortcomings. We will do our best, learn our lessons, grow and keep love coming from inside of us.

As we quiet our world and turn inward, we experience more and more of the power that is within and is the source for everything in our world, indeed the universe. In pursuing this we are asked to believe in what we cannot see, but for me it is like with every step I am returning to something I somehow already know and it all feels so right and natural. It all makes sense and fits, where what I have experienced in the past does not. In acknowledging our connection to our power and our ability to conserve and control how it is used, we open ourselves to the flow of our desires from the unmanifest to the manifest. Remember, the Source is within us. The channel for our flow is what shows up outside. It is the means by which we receive, such as our jobs, people in our lives, all that outside stuff. But these things are *not* our Source. They just represent the ways we receive our desires. Got it? You have to get this! It is essential to your ability to receive what you want. Putting your attention on these things takes your attention off your Source and remember, you get what your attention is on. Now, I'm not saying you don't pay attention to your job, or your relationships! I am saying, do not look to these things as a *source* of your desires. Do not put your attention on these things as the source. Just accept them as the way some of your desires are manifesting. I know this can sound a little confusing, but just take some time if you are having some hesitation. Ask spirit for a little help. Spirit loves it when you ask for help.

So, your Source is within. The power is a part of your

being. You can explore ways to know this power, to conserve it and use it for your benefit. You can realize that you do create your world and you have the power and ability to make it whatever you choose. But in order to take full advantage of it, you have to be willing to give up your old limiting habits, to take a few chances, to leave your comfort zone, to not be afraid of the unknown, and put yourself out there, vulnerable, trusting......knowing spirit is always there to catch you. Or you can choose the world as it is. To me it's a no-brainer.

CHAPTER FIVE

Are You Working With Your Desires or Against Them?

What I am observing in this country and the world as a whole is lack. We believe that there is lack, that there is not enough, that there won't be enough, that some people have more than they should and because of this the rest of us don't have enough. Until we come to an understanding that this is all just an illusion, that we are creating lack through our belief in it, it will continue. Just because the rest of the world believes this and accepts it as fact, does not mean we have to. We can create our own abundance independent of what the rest of the world is doing.

Everything that we are experiencing now was created by our thoughts in the past. So if it is our intention to have things be different in the future, we must stop dwelling on what is, what was, and put our attention on what we want. We must stop reacting to every little thing that occurs. Our reaction dictates our happiness or negativity. We now realize we cannot control the outside world, but we can control our reaction to it. For example: you get a surprise bill in the mail and it's not in your budget. Your first reaction might be: "Oh no! I don't have the money for this. Why did it have to come now? I had other things planned to spend my money on. Now I have to put off my vacation. Woe is me!" These are the very types of thoughts that keep us from getting into the flow of abundance in our lives. Instead of that type of reaction, try something like: "Oh well, here's a little surprise. I'll pay what I can now and wait for the rest of the money to arrive. I know it will. It always does." So if you have the money, pay it all, if not, pay what you can, and know that the void caused by the spending of the money will be filled again as long as you believe it will.

Money is just a form of energy. It is the form that is used today to compensate us for the energy we expend in our lives. Like all energy it needs to flow in order to exist. Holding onto it, fearing losing it, only stifles its flow. You have to allow it to flow to you, allow it to flow out from you and know that the flow is endless, as is all energy in the universe. What you believe becomes your reality. If you have been taught there is a scarcity of money, there will be. You can choose to know there is an endless supply and you can choose to tap into it.

Now I do not want to make money too important here. It is not the money that is important in itself; it is the experiences that it can bring to you. In the world as it is today it takes money to buy experiences. There is all this focus on wealth. That having lots of money can get you what you want. That getting what you want will make you happy. The saying that money cannot buy happiness is true. It can only buy you experiences that may or may not make you feel happy, but they are only temporary. We are beings that are meant to have abundance and there is no reason whatsoever that we cannot have abundance and be happy too. Just don't confuse the two. Don't put dollars ahead of your happiness. We don't need money to be happy, but we do need to be happy to truly enjoy our money. We all want and deserve pleasures. Money is what it takes to get many of them. Just don't put all the importance on *getting* the money. Put the importance on realizing where it materializes from in the first place: Your True Source - You! It can be a little confusing because I say you get what you put your attention on, and so you may be thinking if you put your attention on money then you should get some. The problem arises for most of us in our attitude or how we *feel* when we think of money. Our feelings, through our internal dialog, create our vibrations, which in turn determines what we draw to ourselves. Sadly, many of us do not think of money in a positive manner and do not even realize it.

Learning to think of money in a positive manner depends on your background, upbringing, and where you find yourself at the present moment. If you come from a poor background, you may have been taught there is never enough, and if that is where your interpretation is now, you have a longer road to travel to prosperity than someone who was raised with lots of money and never experienced much lack. But just because someone comes from a background of money does not mean they don't have a poverty consciousness. Even those with lots of money can have the fear that there is not enough to fill their needs and that it may somehow get used up. And on the other side of the coin are those raised with very little but made to feel there is plenty to fulfill the needs of today and tomorrow there will be more coming. Those are actually more fortunate in my way of thinking than some who have come from money but do not have a healthy attitude towards it. So just being wealthy does not mean you have a wealth consciousness. I can think of several people who have lots of money but pinch every penny, are cheap tippers, and quite selfish with their money. Money is meant to be spent and shared for the good of all. It is meant to bring happiness both to the giver and receiver. If you cannot use it in that manner, then you can have a ton of it and you will never be happy. Money is just the means to the end; it is not the substance of abundance. That substance comes from inside of you. How much abundance flows in your life is not determined by the dollars you have. It is determined by whether you have a wealth consciousness or poverty consciousness. And that is determined by your understanding of your abilities to create you own future.

Sharing is an important part of wealth consciousness. If you are not able to share what you have, you demonstrate your belief that there is not enough. And if that is what you are feeling, then that is what you will get – not enough. If we are able to give that which we are seeking for ourselves, no matter what that might be, it is a very powerful way of demonstrating our belief that there is enough, that more is always on the way to us, and that supply in not limited. The more you give, the more you will receive. Even if you are experiencing a shortage now, you can prove your belief that more is coming by sharing what you do have. To enrich the feeling even more, try giving a little bit more than you think you can afford. This sharing need not be in the form of money. It can be material things, kind words, a helping hand, and even kind thoughts and prayers. But it must come from love and gratitude. A word of caution here; your sharing must come from the heart. If it is calculated in order to get more for yourself, then the energy is not right and you are doing a dis-service to all. Not to mention that it won't work.

Let's get back to our thoughts and attitudes creating our experience. In order to create the experiences we want we have to be aware in each moment of our internal dialog and feelings. When we are not aware in the moment, we keep creating more of the same because our attention is not on changing things. We are caught up in the way things are now. If we stay there then we create more of the same and more of the same. So if you want something different for your future you have to make the effort to change the way you are thinking in the present. There is no way to get around this, so you might as well start working on it right now. If you are not in control of your thoughts, if you allow negativity and you are thinking of what you do not want, you are going to keep getting just that.

If we accept where we are now, which we might as well because we cannot change the present, only the future, and put our attention on how we intend things to be and keep our thoughts positive in nature, we can and will change our world. Our goal is to catch our negative habits and replace them with positive ones. If we can spend over 50% of our time thinking positive thoughts and about what we are intending, do you see that is going to get us better results than spending over 50% of our time on the other side of the scale? So it is our goal to keep raising the percentage of time spent on the good stuff and gradually do away with all the garbage. We cannot expect to be positive 100% of the time, after all we are only humans, but we can do our very best. And our best will get better with practice.

This pertains to all things in our life whether it is wealth, a successful career, a love relationship, our health, you name it. You get what you spend your time thinking about. If your relationship is suffering and you spend your time frustrated about it you will continue the cycle. Same goes for your job, your bank account, and your health. We cannot tell ourselves it's okay to be unhappy with our job right now, to feel broke right now, to feel ill right now, or be without love and feel lonely right now. It's not okay. None of it is okay. Yes, we have to accept this moment as it is, but it does not have to be okay with us. Can you see the point I am trying to make here? If we attract by what we are thinking and feeling, can you see where this attitude will only bring more of the same to you? When you are focused on what is and that is not what you want, you are only creating more of the same. What we must do is find the positive in the moment and keep our intention for what we *do* want upper most in our minds. So the job you have now is not your ideal. It does bring you money to pay the bills and get you by while you are working on having your ideal job. You do not have as much money as you would like, but you can enjoy what you do have and be grateful for it. If your health is not so great, you can focus on ways to get and feel better, rather than on the discomfort you are feeling. If you are without a wanted relationship, or the one you do have is suffering, you can think about what you want in a mate or concentrate on ways to make your existing relationship more fulfilling for both of you. Or better still; if you just work on being happy where you are now and make the most of it, most of these things will eventually fall into place. I know I am a starting to sound like a broken record with all this repeating myself, but it is so important that you get this into your consciousness and understanding. By making the most of each moment, each day, we are not resisting, and when we are not resisting, it conserves our energy and allows for the positive to flow into our life. If you wait for your job, money, a relationship, or your body to make you happy, you will never be. Dr. Wayne Dyer says, "Love what you do and do what you love." If you are not able to do what you love right now, find a way to love what you are doing. The best way to do that is to get in touch with the spirit that lives within you and allow it to guide you.

What we are living and what we believe are intertwined. This book is meant to assist you in changing your beliefs and habits, or modifying them, and understanding how we can create a world more to our liking and live the life we dream of. If you base your tomorrows on what you know from your yesterdays, your tomorrows will be just like yesterday. So unless you are thrilled with your past experiences, you need to leave that realm of what you know and go to a realm of something different – perhaps the unknown, the unfamiliar, to be open to new things, uncertainty, a place where all things are possible. Like booking a trip on the starship Enterprise! If you remain attached to your past, your future will be just a repetition of it. So be bold and step into that arena where things are not prearranged, where uncertainty is the word of the day, and allow yourself to be insecure for a while. This is where freedom lives.

Allow for the potentiality of new and exciting manifestations. Get out of your rut and start *living* your life! We don't dwell on the past and we don't write a strict outline for the future. We just put what we want out there and wait to see what fun and exciting ways the universe (or God-they are one) will find to present them to us. Intend for the *feeling* of what you want without putting restrictions on how it will appear. Be spontaneous and open to new ideas and opportunities when they do appear. Be aware of the world around you and watch for signs and clues. If we are preoccupied worrying about things not going as we want, we can miss opportunities being presented to us. The universe can be very subtle. Who knows? Perhaps something even better is on the way. Follow your heart, not your ego.

Attachment to the outcome limits your creative abilities and limits what the universe is able to send to you. If you have a rigid idea of what you want and how you want it, it makes it very difficult for energy to flow efficiently and freely. If you are thinking about what you want from the stand point of, "When will it get here?" or "Why isn't it here yet?" or

"Am I really able to create what I really want? If so, where is it?"- your attention is on the lack of it being here and doubt. If that is what you are thinking and feeling, that is what you will get...doubt and the lack of your desires. Becoming detached from the outcome once we introduce our desires/intentions to the "universal pool" is essential to our success. We can make our intentions known as many times as we like as long as we simply ask for it and then let all other thoughts of it go and go about our business. The best time to place our orders to the "pool" is during our meditations or quiet times, while the mind is silent and we are in contact with our inner Self. Dwelling on whatever it is, usually leads to doubt or some sort of negative thinking. So just be unbending in your intention to have it without becoming obsessed about when and how. If you do want to think about your intentions during the day, just be sure you are thinking, "yes, I will be getting a new car" and not "where is my new car?" We have to trust that whatever we have asked for will come to us in the appropriate form and at the appropriate time. Let the universe surprise you. I am going to talk more about drawing what you want to your experience in the next chapter, so for now I just want to emphasize that you learn to detach yourself and go about your life, staying in the moment, finding happiness where you are, while you wait for your desires to manifest.

Detachment does not only pertain to your personal endeavors. It also pertains to the world around you. All the things that are happening in this world are not your responsibility. You do not have to become so involved that it becomes a part of your emotional experience. Everything is as it is. Everything for everybody is as it is. You cannot change what already is. You can feel compassion, you can send love, you can send healing, but you do not have to make it a part of you. Mind your own business and fix your own life! Let others mind their own business and fix their own lives. If asked you may offer guidance, but let each find their own answers, just as you must find your own.

CHAPTER SIX

Survival Among the Masses

Our happiness or unhappiness, negativity, is the result of our reactions to the world around us. As previously stated, we cannot control the outside world, but we can control our reactions to it. We can choose to let our buttons be pushed and relinquish our control or we can choose to change the way we see things and therefore our reactions to them. This requires some discipline, which we have talked about, and the willingness on our part to be open and experiment.

Energy, or God if you like, is impartial. It seeks no particular result. We direct it by what we are, how we are feeling. For example, if you want abundance but do not feel abundant, instead you feel your lack, you cannot expect to get that which you do not reflect out. It is universal law: like attracts like. Your desires can only manifest themselves at the level of your vibration, or what you allow yourself. You may think you do not limit yourself, but if you take a closer look at your attitudes and beliefs you will find just how much you actually do. We must learn to become limitless in our attitudes and thinking. God is limitless and being a part of God makes us also limitless. When we are asking for our desires to manifest for us, we must to learn to *feel* what this desire is going to feel like when it arrives. We *feel* it in order to bring it to us. We align ourselves with that energy, that power, which manifests everything. Then we carry the knowing that it is on its way to us as we detach ourselves and go about our daily lives being aware of the world around us for clues and signs of actions we are to take.

So how do we know if we are on the right track? We have been provided with an extremely effective system to assist us. It lies inside each of us. It is the feeling or response we have in the form of a sensation. Some call it our "gut", but for most it lies in the area of the heart or solar plexus. When you want to know if something is right or not, simply ask your question to your God-Self and wait for the response. It can be ever so faint or hit you like a bulldozer. But it is there inside of you. If you feel good or comfortable, then proceed. If you feel uncomfortable or uncertain then this is not the right time. Be sure you focus inside and not let your mind, or ego, interfere. It can be very tricky and it may take some practice to know just who is communicating with you. If you are in doubt at all, simply wait. Take no action. Come back to it later if the need be or let it go. If it is meant to be it will come back to you later on.

Part of being in flow is releasing our need for control, relinquishing resistance, and knowing what effort and action mean. We are willing to put out the effort to master our disciplines, but we do not become obsessed with them. By this I mean we come from a place of quiet desire and a loving heart. We do things because we want to and it feels good when we do. Our lives are better when we do. We take action when we feel the time is right. We do not come from a calculating stance that if we make ourselves do these things we will get what we want. And we are going to make it work if it kills us! When we come from that space we are putting out way too much effort and pushing too hard. The energy we generate is not right and things just won't work. We instead relax and enjoy our spiritual times and *pull or draw* things to us instead of trying to push our energy out there. Again, it is about aligning ourselves to the vibration of what we seek. Let go of all your stresses. Your outer world is a reflection of the inner you, so become serene and watch how your outer world changes. Remain in a state of grace.

Just because others believe certain things does not mean you have to. I am going to talk about health issues, but the gist of this pertains to most everything. Let's say for example you're a male and most of the males in your family have contracted prostate cancer. You do not have to believe you will get it. It is your choice what you believe and your choice how you *think* about your health. You can think, "My chances of not getting it are pretty slim" or you can think, "I am perfectly healthy. Every part of my Being is healthy." Even if you are not perfectly healthy in this moment, it is better to proclaim your health than to think negative thoughts about it. By focusing on a healthy body you are drawing health to you. Be careful how your dialogue runs though. You do not want to think, "I will not get cancer" or "I will not be a victim of 'such and such'" because if you will recall, the universe doesn't pick up on the 'not'. It hears cancer or 'such and such' and that is what you will get! Also, do not put your desires off into the future by saying, "I will have perfect health" or "I will have "such and such." That dialogue keeps things in the future. Stay in the present tense with all your thoughts and you will do fine.

Even when you are sick you can make the most of it or you can wallow in your misery and make it worse. You can find ways to help yourself. Now I know when you are suffering from the flu and feeling nauseated it is difficult to be cheery. But you can think about how it feels to be well and look forward to your feeling better. You can try to distract yourself from your suffering by listening to music or watching a little television. Anything but dwelling on how awful you feel. That goes for any affliction. Keep your focus on good health and you will find yourself being healthier. You will avoid colds, the flu, etc. You can even go so far as to talk to germs when you feel yourself coming down with something. You can tell them they are not welcome here and that you will not give into their plans for you, so they might as well just go away. Don't scoff! It can work!

Especially with a little practice.

One thing we have not discussed much is gratitude. Be grateful for whatever is good in your life. Be grateful and share what you do have whether it be a little or a lot. No matter your circumstances, you do have things to be grateful for. We should even be grateful for the times things didn't turn out so hot because those times offer us the lessons we need to grow and evolve. Also be grateful in advance for those things you have asked for. Thanking God, or the universe, for what is on its way to you is very empowering. It demonstrates your belief in your Self and reinforces your magnetism for drawing them to you. We can come to a point in our life where we are feeling fulfilled with things the way they are. We haven't stopped desiring things, we are just grateful for what is and enjoying what is. If you can feel this way in your experience, then the abundance, the affluence, you seek will follow. You have cleared the way for it.

If we seek abundance, affluence, money, before 'our house is in order' we will find it doesn't work well. Many of us have been down that road and are still trying to work that system. It requires a lot of hard work and many times fails. Things seem to pass us by or slip through our fingers. We push to try to make things happen. Instead we don't give up our desires. We still have our intentions for success, abundance, to be fulfilled in every way. But our day-to-day goal is to find fulfillment in each moment. To be able to love and share and be grateful and know everything is coming to us in the right time.

I would like to share with you what lead me to write this book. I wanted to let you know it takes patience with yourself in order to succeed. It takes trial and error. It takes commitment. I'm sure there are many of you out there like me who want results and want them *now.* I have made some 'leaps' in my quest and many accomplishments as I look back. There have also been times though when I felt I wasn't moving forward fast enough and found myself frustrated with what I felt were my shortcomings. As I went along I finally came to realize that I could only progress at the rate that my belief system allowed me. Let me explain what that means: your old belief system is a part of your being. You just accept without thinking that things are a certain way – the way you were taught they were. And because they are a part of you, they are so. Now you are exploring new beliefs and though you may believe your new Truths, they have not yet become a part of your *knowing*. They are not yet a natural part of you: just as you know when you break a fingernail it will grow back; when you inhale your lungs will fill with air, and in the *world vision* if you hang out with people who have colds you will get a cold. You don't really think about it, it just is. That is the point we need to reach with our new Truths before we really see how powerful we are. They not only become our beliefs, they become *our knowing*, a part of us. Give yourself time and give yourself credit for what you have accomplished and never expect more than what you are in this moment. Intend for more, but accept where you are. In this you find your success.

We are here to serve humanity and grow. When you find your place in this service then joy, fulfillment, and abundance will flow to you. For as you give of yourself, your energy, so this energy shall be returned to you multiplied many times. In the system of today's world this exchange of energy returns to us mostly in the form of money. It is the energy behind your giving, your service, that determines your return. How is your energy being spent? If you are not getting the results you want, perhaps you should examine where and how you are spending your energy.

Now let's not kid ourselves that life is going to be perfect. At least it's not going to seem perfect to us on the earth plane. It's all an illusion anyway, but that's not how it feels sometimes. We can be going along doing our best, thinking we are on track with our spiritual practices, working on loving, caring and sharing when all of sudden our life gets turned upside down. We have our hearts broken, are punched in the gut and left wondering what happened and why. We can search ourselves for answers and others may give us their opinions on the reasons for our grief and turmoil. But nothing comforts us. Our pain can be so intense we can hardly stand it. We ask ourselves where is our spiritual strength and how could this happen? We may feel disappointed and lost. We may feel anger. It is all part of our growth whether we like it or not. We are here to experience being human and we just have to hang in there and not give up on ourselves, allow ourselves to feel our emotions and let them flow through us. It's okay to be pissed off, to feel grief, just don't hang onto those feelings too long. Come back to your Self as soon as you can and keep going, for the ultimate goal is still ahead.

No matter what is going on with the masses, we can live the life of our dreams. We just need to turn our attention to, and make our commitment to, making the changes necessary in our own lives in order to become one with Spirit. It is individual. And the individuals make up the whole. If we can touch others in a way that inspires them to find their own Truth then we have contributed to journey of mankind back to Self. We have added more light to our planet.

CHAPTER SEVEN

Putting It All Together

While you are building your relationship with spirit, also build a new relationship with your body, especially if you are lacking good health, energy and strength. It is the vessel that carries you through this life experience, so you better take care of it if you want it to give you good service throughout your life. If you plan to keep your automobile for a long time, you service it; maintain it for a long life. Do the same for your body. You cannot trade it in for a new one if you wear it out. The same goes for your mind.

Now I would like to summarize some of the suggestions I've made and add some more for creating a healthy mind, body, and spirit – for a whole you – happy, healthy and robust.

To care for spirit, take time everyday to honor the Self within. Find a quiet place where you will not be disturbed, preferably for at least 20 minutes, shut off the mind, relax and join with spirit. You can play some music if this helps you relax and quiet yourself. You can listen to narrated meditations. You can do this by yourself, or with another or others. It seems to be best if you close your eyes so there are no distractions. Focusing on deep breaths and complete exhales is also helpful. Allow yourself to leave everything behind and float away to wherever your heart/spirit takes you.

Another extremely beneficial discipline is to spend time in nature. Whether it is in the neighborhood park or you can really get out into the country. Just do it regularly. If you are in the city, plan some extended trips (some call them vacations) to the ocean, mountains, desert, lake, river, whatever you fancy. Your connection to nature and our planet is fundamental and the benefits empowering.

The mind gets some R&R while you are with spirit, but there are other things you can do also. Humor is great. Watch funny movies and love stories with happy endings, read books that make you feel good. Have relaxing conversations with friends. Go to special places – nice restaurants, the theater if that's something you enjoy, museums, galleries, whatever. Having a hobby you enjoy is great for your mind, also. Use your imagination. So long as it feels good and brings you joy.

Now for the body. There are two parts to this. What you put in it and what you do with it. I'm a retired personal trainer but I'm not going to get all strict and overbearing about this. Just be sensible. You are what you eat; so if you don't want to look like a donut, don't eat one. Your body has essential needs to rebuild and repair itself for a long, healthy and agile life. Fish and chips and burgers and fries, and pizza are not on the list! Not that you cannot enjoy your favorite decadence from time to time, just don't make grease and sugar your mainstay if you want to feel good and look good.

Eat breakfast! Even if it is just some fruit or juice and piece of toast, bagel or English muffin. I have a banana, tofu, yogurt, orange juice and soymilk shake I make that is delicious and fills my requirements. Hey, even my husband likes it! The point is to get something in your stomach in the morning. If you love breakfast, good for you. Watch out for sugary cereals, and bacon and eggs are okay for a treat, but not too often. The rest of the day you should get some fruit and vegetables and some protein in the form of meat or tofu (soy) or rice and beans, and some carbohydrates such as pasta, etc. Your proportions should be approximately 50% carbs, 30% fat and 20% proteins. It is best to select fresh foods whenever possible and frozen is a good second choice. There are lots of books out there and this one is not about quality eating, so I'll leave it up to you to make your commitment to this discipline, which I realize is quite difficult for many. If you're going to commit to spiritual quest you might as well do it all the way.

The second part is exercise. Now before you start groaning and moaning, it's not all that bad. Walk everyday, if you can, for at least 30 minutes, 60 is better. If you do not have a block of time that size you can break it into two sessions. Doesn't matter how it gets done as long as it gets done. You don't have to go running or buy an exercise cycle or some other type of machine. If you want to and *will use it*, go ahead. Also find a sport you enjoy – racquetball, tennis, basketball, softball, bowling, kick boxing, dance class, whatever. As long as you're moving, you're using muscles and burning calories. You should participate on a regular basis so your body gets used to what you're asking of it. This will mean less sore muscles and less chance for injury. Some kind of resistance training (that means weights) is also necessary to maintain muscle mass and tone, especially as we mature. You don't need to go for the Mr. Olympia look, just tone up those flabby muscles. While you strengthen your muscles, you also strengthen your bone mass. So there is double benefit there for you. You will enjoy more energy and better health. This is especially important in our senior years, so take care of your body. As I said, you cannot trade it in for a new one when it deteriorates to mush. Again, there is a lot of information out there on this, so you have no excuse.

Other things you may like to look into if you have not already are alternative health care, bodywork and all forms of natural healing. Acupuncture, rolfing, massage therapy, Reiki, reflexology, polarity work and naturopaths are just a few. Get chemicals out of your healthcare regimen whenever possible and safe (be sure to check with your physician before changing medications if you are regularly taking a prescription for something). Using natural substances for healing is much easier on your body. I am not giving medical advice in any fashion, only listing some suggestions for you to think about. Any changes in your regimen should be done under the supervision of your healthcare professional.

Another very interesting subject is Feng Shui: the placement and arrangement of things to allow for the maximum influence of Chi energy. I personally have had some very interesting experiences with this. Read some books or attend a workshop.

Some other ideas to make our life and environment enjoyable include having fresh flowers in you home and/or office all year round, playing pleasant music in the background while you are working around your home, and taking some time every once in awhile to experience complete silence while being completely aware. (This requires you to turn off your phone!) I find this works best a night, because the world outside is quieter and the dark adds to the mood of silence. Being out under the stars is nice also, but enjoying a beautiful view in silence in the daylight can also bring you inner peace. Next time you start to turn on the television for entertainment, think about reading or listening to a book on tape instead. I'm not putting down television for all those who think it's great, but don't use it to escape your responsibility to yourself. I am suggesting that you vary your activities and not get in a rut that keeps you from exploring other possibilities for yourself. You can use your own imagination to create more peace and quiet in your life. It's all up to you!

I also like affirmations, or notes you put up to see each day. These messages to yourself should be changed on a regular basic, because after a short time we tend to not see or notice them anymore. You can write your own from books you read or videos you watch, or lectures you attend. You can buy books that are mostly affirmations. Here is a list of some you may like. Some are my own words and some I have borrowed from my many teachers. I thank them now for their influence in my life.

Before I start the list I would like to say we are all here for a purpose. We came into this human body for a purpose. We are here to serve mankind and this planet. Each morning get out of bed with a grateful attitude and thank God for all that is good in your life, for this new day, for another chance to experience the wonder of this planet and ask, "What can I do to be of service today?"

Okay, now the list:

Good Morning God!

...Dr. Wayne Dyer

Where Are Your Thoughts?

You Are What You Think About

I Remember Who I Am

I Am Eternal, Immortal, Universal, and Infinite.

My Expectations Are Truly Limitless

...Stuart Wilde

I Create My World. I Have the Power to Make it Whatever I Choose.

Today I Shall Judge Nothing that Occurs
...A Course in Miracles

Today I Will Honor All Living Things

Today I Will Not Give into Anger
...Principles of Reiki

I Can Love Unconditionally

I Am the Best I Can Be and I Love Myself Unconditionally

Today I will give to everyone I meet, whether it be a smile or a prayer or a compliment.
...Deepak Chopra

I Honor My True Self At All Times

I Will Be Impeccable With My Word

...don Miguel Ruiz

Today I Feel Gratitude For All Things in My Life

...Principles of Reiki

I Release My Need to Be in Control

I Accept Each Moment As It Is

I Will Pay Attention to the Choices I Make
in Every Moment of My Day

... Deepak Chopra

Money is not My Supply.
The Divine Within Me is My Supply.

...John Randolph Price

The Basis of My Life is Freedom;
the Purpose of My Life is Joy

... Abraham-Hicks

have tried to give credit where credit is due here, but the messages are the same, so much is repeated from teacher to teacher.

An alternative way to use your affirmations, or notes, is to pick seven, one for each day of the week. Then you read the one for the day upon rising, at lunchtime, a few other times during the day whenever you can, and before you go to bed.

It is also very helpful to keep a journal of your thoughts and insights. When you look back over them later on, you will see how your thinking has progressed. You will probably be surprised at how much your thinking has changed without your realizing it. Keeping a journal can be quite inspiring. Without one it is difficult to keep track of your progress. You can also ask spirit to speak through your writing and that is totally awesome. Get quiet and ask for spirit to communicate through your writing. Then just write whatever comes into your thoughts without editing or thinking. Just write. You can rewrite it later so it is legible if you are handwriting, but do not change any of it.

You may want to set boundaries for your life experience. This is done by taking a blank piece of paper and drawing a circle on it. Inside this circle you write down all the things you are willing to allow in your life. Some examples are: success, love, abundance, health, you get the picture. Anything not written in your circle is not welcome in your life. Review this circle each day and re-affirm your boundaries. As time goes on you will probably think of new things to write within your sacred circle.

Another fun thing to do is to start a network of good deeds. It works like the film "Pay It Forward," or network marketing, if you know how it works. Here's an example: the first week you pick up a piece of litter twice a day, everyday for the full week. At the end of the week you have two of your friends commit to doing this same thing everyday for an entire week. It is very important that you pick two people you trust to follow through with it. At the end of their week they each have two of their friends commit to the same thing everyday for a full week. At the end of that week each of them passes it on to two more people and so on. Can you see where this could go? It can be fabulous! So please give it a whirl. It is so much fun, does so much good and you feel so good because of it. Now you and your friends can continue with this even after you pass it on or you can start a new one, such as complimenting a stranger everyday for a full week. You can come up with all sorts of good ideas.

Remember at the beginning of the book I said I would explain the difference between something giving you pleasure and happiness. In case you forgot or haven't figured it out yet, having lots of money or someone to love or a good job or taking an awesome vacation, can all give you pleasure, but not necessarily happiness. Happiness comes from *inside* of you and pleasure is supplied outside of you. Pleasures are superficial; happiness is a part of your being.

With everything that is going on around us and all the things that are pulling at us for attention, it is easy to be distracted from our goals and commitments. It takes a strong will to stay with it. It depends on just how much you want to be in a better place and how much respect you have for yourself. If you follow the suggestions I have made, your self- respect will increase. Our ego can be quite good at hiding our lack of self-respect, but many of us suffer from it. If you get distracted, just come back to it and keep coming back. It will soon become too important for you not to be committed to your quest. The difference in the way you feel and how your world feels will mean everything to you.

Money does not measure who you are or your success. You'll know you're where you want to be when you are living you life, feeling *truly* happy, and you realize you don't need those other things you thought would make you happier. It's not that you no longer want them, but you realize you don't *need* them to feel happy and fulfilled. You don't really need to have that certain car, or that house, or that special vacation or that better job. Those things are nice and you still want them, but *you feel great right now even without them.* Those things are nice and will bring you pleasure and we all deserve pleasure, but they are not going to make you happy or fulfilled. When you reach that point where you are happy and the things you do and have are just to give you pleasure, you are bringing heaven to earth. And from that point all the good things in life you have been wanting just seem to flow to you.

So there you have it. Some disciplines I feel are necessary in our journey to wholeness, oneness and wellness. I wish you love and success and the ability to try and try again. For this life is a journey from where we ever find ourselves now to wherever we end up in the end. There is no single destination. No point where we can say, "Well, this is it. I have grown all I can. Now I will stop and just be here." We stop this experience when we cross over. What we are all searching for is happiness. It comes from within.........God is with, and in you.....always.

Deepak Chopra quotes Austrian poet and philosopher Franz Kafka in his book "The Seven Spiritual Laws of Success." I find myself coming back to this time and time again.

"You need not leave your room. Remain sitting at your table and listen. You need not even listen, simply wait. You need not even wait, just learn to become quiet, and still, and solitary. The world will freely offer itself to you to be unmasked. It has no choice; it will roll in ecstasy at your feet."

*To **know** the Truth is to **be** the truth.*
It is all here. Always was.
Always will be.
The secret of life is opening your awareness
and allowing yourself to receive
all Life has to offer.

Original Source of Creation,
The Void of All That Is.
Thank you for the breath of life,
Thank you for my gifts...

...

Jamie Sams, from
"Sacred Path Cards"

ABOUT THE AUTHOR

Mary Lou Morris was born in Australia. As a child, she came to the United States, where she has lived most of her life. Like her parents, who were somewhat "gypsies," she too has spent most of her life moving around the northwest with her husband.

After settling into their own little piece of heaven in northwest Montana, she was guided to share with others, through this book, what she found brings peace and fulfillment to her life. In her travels, she had the opportunity to try quite a few different jobs: pushing burgers, bookkeeper, bank teller, bartender. The majority of her time was spent in the medical field, finally turning to alternative medical practices and physical well-being. She became a personal trainer, wellness counselor, Reiki Master and also works with energy healing.

She is forever thankful to the teachers along her pathway. Mary Lou hopes that through her own writing she can assist others to discover the answers that she found bring a little bit of heaven to our life journey.

-MLM

To order additional copies of
Getting Everything You Want....,
please complete the order blank below (or a copy),
mail with your check or m.o. for $11.95 plus s/h to:
ONE STEP CLOSER
PO Box 888, Libby, MT 59923
email: onestepclosermt@juno.com

Order Blank
ONE STEP CLOSER
PO Box 888, Libby MT 59923

Name:______________________________________

Address:____________________________________

City, State, Zip:_______________________________

Daytime phone_________________________________

____Copies of
Getting Everything You Want
@ $11.95 each:_______________

Shipping/handling, first book @ S/H
$2.____________
.50 for each additional book ____________

Total________________

e-mail: onestepclosermt@juno.com

THANK YOU!